Watching the Seasons

Winter

by Emily C. Dawson

Bullfrog Books

Ideas for Parents and Teachers

Bullfrog Books let children practice nonfiction reading at the earliest reading levels. Repetition, familiar words, and photo labels support early readers. Here are some tips for reading with children.

Before Reading
- Discuss the cover photo. What does it tell them?

- Look at the picture glossary together. Read and discuss the words.

Read the Book
- "Walk" through the book and look at the photos. Let the child ask questions. Point out the photo labels.

- Read the book to the child, or have him or her read independently.

After Reading
- Prompt the child to think more. Ask: What is winter like where you live? What do you like to do in winter?

Bullfrog Books are published by Jump!
5357 Penn Ave. South, Minneapolis, MN 55419
www.jumplibrary.com

Library of Congress Cataloging-in-Publication Data
Dawson, Emily C.
  Winter / by Emily C. Dawson.
  p. cm. — (Watching the seasons) (Bullfrog books)
Summary: "This photo-illustrated book for early readers describes how winter weather affects the actions of animals, the growth of plants, and the activities of people. Includes photo glossary" --Provided by publisher.
Includes bibliographical references and index.
Audience: Grades K-3.
ISBN 978-1-62031-017-5 (hbk.)
1. Winter--Juvenile literature. I. Title.
QB637.8.D29 2013
508.2--dc23
                                  2012009120

Series Editor: Rebecca Glaser
Series Designer: Ellen Huber
Photo Researcher: Heather Dreisbach

Photo Credits
All photos by Shutterstock except: Alamy, 6; Dreamstime, 3a, 3b, 5, 7, 16, 19, 23a, 23b, 23f; Getty Images, 4, 20; SuperStock, 11, 17, 18, 23d

Printed in the United States of America at Corporate Graphics in North Mankato, Minnesota.
7-2012 / 1124
10 9 8 7 6 5 4 3 2 1

Table of Contents

Winter is Quiet

In winter, nature is quiet.

Trees are bare. Snowflakes fall.

In winter,
cardinals fly.
They do not
mind the snow.

In winter,
animals sleep.

8

A bat hibernates. It sleeps all winter.

In winter,
night is long.
The sun sets early.

whiteout

In winter, wind whips snow.

It is a whiteout.

It is hard to see in a blizzard.

In winter,
icicles form.

14

Drip! Drip!

Snow melts in the sun.

Cold air freezes the water.

sand

In winter, roads get icy.
Plows spread sand.
It helps car tires grip.

In winter,
ponds freeze.

Julia ice-skates.

She plays hockey
with her brother.

In winter, kids sled. Ito and Uki race down the hill. Ito wins. What do you do in winter?

Watching the Seasons

Spring

Summer

Winter

Fall

Picture Glossary

blizzard
A heavy snowstorm with wind speeds of at least 35 miles per hour (56 k/m).

hockey
A game played on ice with sticks and a puck that skaters try to hit into the other team's net.

freeze
To become solid or turn into ice when the air is very cold.

icicle
A long, thin piece of ice formed from dripping water that froze.

hibernate
To go into a deep sleep for the purpose of saving energy when there is not much food and it is cold.

whiteout
When blowing snow makes it impossible to see because everything looks white.

Index

To Learn More

Learning more is as easy as 1, 2, 3.

1) Go to www.factsurfer.com

2) Enter "winter" into the search box.

3) Click the "Surf" button to see a list of websites.

With factsurfer.com, finding more information is just a click away.